T0196563

You Ought
to get to
Know Him

WHO?

Verda Sherrod

Order this book online at www.trafford.com
or email orders@trafford.com

Most Trafford titles are also available at major online book retailers.

Unless otherwise indicated, all Scripture quotations are taken from the King James Version of the Bible.

Printed in the United States of America.

ISBN: 978-1-4669-4628-6 (sc)
ISBN: 978-1-4669-4627-9 (e)

Trafford rev. 08/16/2012

 www.trafford.com

North America & international
toll-free: 1 888 232 4444 (USA & Canada)
phone: 250 383 6864 ✦ fax: 812 355 4082

DEDICATION

Never forget to be truthful and kind. Hold these virtues tightly. Write them deep within your heart. If you want favor with both God and man, and a reputation for good judgment and common sense, then trust the Lord completely; don't ever trust yourself. In everything you do, put God first, and he will direct you and crown your efforts with success. (Proverbs 3:3-6, TLBP).

This book is dedicated first to my Lord, God, and Savior. Secondly, it is dedicated to a man who became a new creation in Christ, my late husband, father of my children, my best friend and companion, Orville Walter Sherrod, Jr. After he got saved, he became a dedicated husband and a devoted Christian that loved the Lord God with all his heart, with all his soul, and with all his mind (Matthew 22:37). He loved God with all his being and he demonstrated it daily by studying and meditating on the word. Not only did he meditate on the word; he shared the word with everyone he talked to. He was a doer of the word. He was a man who pushed his way beyond physical strength to do what the Lord said do. I appreciate the 26 years we spent together.

Sherrod was truly one of a kind. I am thankful that he taught me about Christ through his actions and deeds. I see his reflection in all that I do. When I find something that reminds me of him, I either laugh until I cry or cry until I laugh. Love makes the difference. Thank you for the journey. "When a good man dies, he leaves an inheritance to his grandchildren; but when a sinner dies, his wealth is stored up for the godly" (Proverbs 14:22 TLB).

Can you accomplish in death what you desired in life?

As Always,
Verda

To God be the Glory

ACKNOWLEDGMENTS

Thanks to my Lord and Savior, Jesus the Christ. For, it is He who keeps me in perfect peace as I journey through this life. His grace and mercy allow be to see the good in the bad. Thanks to my friends and family and all who encourage me daily. Special thanks to Tracy Bohannon for proof reading the book for me.

To God be the Glory for the Things He's done.

CONTENTS

INTRODUCTION

But be ye doers of the word, and not hearers only, deceiving your souls

(James 1:21, KJV).

Sherrod, it seems like a lifetime, and yet it seems like yesterday when we were together, laughing and talking about everything and nothing. I can still hear clearly and remember your dying words, "You ought to get to know Him". Your last praise and worship was on your deathbed. *The hour is coming, and now is when the true worshipers will worship the Father in spirit and in truth; for the Father is seeking such to worship Him. God is Spirit, and those who worship Him must worship in spirit and truth* (John 4:23-24). On your deathbed you handed me the mantle of responsibility to continue the work that you started . . . Evangelism. Because of your dying words, I am charged to tell everyone I meet everywhere I go, "You ought to get to know Him."

There are many genres to spread the Good News. The ones that I've chosen are through music and through this book. First the poem and the CD that continue the work that Sherrod started, spreading the Gospel. Now it is time for the book. Hopefully, this book will spread the Good News and bring others to Christ, which was Sherrod's desire. When this book is read, the readers will *look into the perfect law of liberty, and continue therein, he being not a forgetful hearer, but a doer of the work, this man shall be blessed in his deed.* Sherrod was one who made a difference in the church, community, at work, and in the lives of others. This book will do likewise.

Proverbs 18:24 (TLBP) There are "friends" who pretend to be friends, but there is a friend who sticks closer than a brother. A man who has friends must himself be friendly.

Sherrod and I had many friends who cared enough to help us during his illness and many recoveries. There are many people deserving of acknowledgment but I fear I will not remember all of them. If so, please understand that trauma can cause forgetfulness. These are they who took Sherrod to his appointments and prepared and brought food to us during his illness. These are they who visited; sat with him in the hospitals; called; allowed me to cry on their shoulders; prayed with and for us; cut the grass, shoveled our snow, cleaned the house, gave encouragement and prayed for us throughout Sherrod's journey.

I must thank the dialysis team of doctors and nurses for the care and love that they gave him. Without a doubt, I must thank Shantena Gilbert, Jeanette Broadway, and Quedellis Greene, for driving Sherrod to his doctor's appointments; James and Darlene Irby, Paul and Paulette Coleman, and Ayumi and Tim Olmstead for sticking closer than a brother in the midst of our pain and suffering. They are the ones that allowed me to cry on their shoulders and grieve. Mrs. Catherine King is a special friend who called Sherrod regularly and helped him to realize how important he was in her life and in the lives of others. When I couldn't get Sherrod to follow doctors' orders, both she and Joyce Hubbard persuaded him to do so, and he liked it.

Special gratitude goes to Pastor Arlene Wyrick, Angela Grant, and Stacy VanDenOever for bringing food to the hospital when hospital staff forgot to feed him. Sincere appreciation goes to Angelique and Adam LeCour and Judi Hetzel for bringing food to the house and for helping me to breathe again when I felt overwhelmed by the turbulence of pain and uncertainty. I will never forget Eric Jackson, Bill and Mary Knapp for coming to the house for Bible studies that encouraged us and lifted our spirits. Bill, thank you for the ramp you provided for Sherrod so that he could get to his car without falling. Having it made it more convenient for Sherrod to get in and out of the house. Your kindness will always be remembered.

I am indebted to Creighton Mabry for calling Sherrod daily to check on and encourage him and make him laugh. You made him laugh a lot. Truly, laughter proved to be the best medicine for Sherrod, because "A merry heart makes a cheerful countenance, But by sorrow of the heart the spirit is broken" (Proverbs 15:13, NKJV).

Thanks to Lurma Greene and Darlene Irby for being more than friends. They were like sisters to Sherrod. Thanks to my sisters, Vertis and Joyce of always praying with and for me. I am especially thankful to Zea'Mya and Imani Willlis, my grandchildren, Casmere Kennedy, Cleashae Crowder, and Aaron Talley and his family for caring enough to visit and spend time with me after Sherrod's death; to (Grandma Kennedy), Sandra Kennedy for allowing the girls to stay with me after Sherrod's death and for remembering to call and encourage me when I felt sad and lost. I am thankful to Erma McGinnis and Dr. Gloria Smith who said "you ought to write a book." I don't think this is what they had in mind, but it is a book, nonetheless.

I am grateful to: Natasha Huntley, without whom I would never have been able to find words to write this book; To Scott McKinney because without him I would not have been able to get out to the public some of the CD's and there would be no cover for the CD. Thanks to Pastor Hess for playing the CD and for allowing me to go on his radio station to make the audience aware of the CD and the book. I am grateful to Ebon Gurley, who tried to talk Sherrod into getting a kidney transplant so that he would not need dialysis; my daughter, Tishajodia Willis-Holmes who laughs and cries with me and shares my burdens; my sisters, Joyce Scott and Vertis Williams who continue to encourage me with God's word; my father, Verdis Scott, who shares his wisdom and love with me; the late Athlene Cotton, and Pearlie Parker for saying, "it's going to be all right baby," and to Toni Clark and Mary Thompson for being just a phone call away.

Thanks to: JoAnn Wellington who prays for me and keeps the Scripture before me daily; Cathy Frierson; Oshie Acrey; Evangelist Emma Pulley; Pastor Furman Robinson; Pastor Geraldine Richardson; Billy and Sylvia Scott; the late Apostle Shirley McClendon, my pastor and confidant; Pastor Ollie Mae Rudolph, who encouraged me to keep a strong upper lip; Kecia Collins; A.J. Jennings; Evelyn Atkinson; Lillie Boyd; Sonja Woodson; Jeff and Lowell McGinnis; Patty Perry; Loretta Whitt; Dr. Hugh and Letha Smith; Dessie Fullerton; Sarah Dyer; Eve LeCour; Johnny Cannon; Dr. Henri Treadwell; Minister Duane Perkins; Margaret Armstrong; Yuvonne Bates; Yvonne Cooper; Shanelle Colen; Angela Glubke; Sheila White; J and Thelma Vaughn; Willie Spraggins; Kathy Scherer; Judi Hetzel, the late Thelma and Barbara Sherrod, who allowed me to vent and never told me to "just get over it; my family; my neighbors in the community; my church, Now Faith Full Gospel Deliverance Ministry, Second Missionary Baptist Church; Shiloh Baptist Church; Macedonia Baptist Church; Lifestyles, and my Stars and Stripes families for being my support system.

Mostly, thank you Sherrod, for speaking life into my life and the lives of others. This book will help all who read it to get to know God more intimately.

Verda Sherrod

ABOUT SHERROD

Sherrod, "Big O," was born to Orville "Buddy" Sherrod and Norma June Wallace-Sherrod. His mother died of Cancer when he was a young child. He watched her suffer but he also watched her study the word with those who came by the house to take care of her. His father taught him about survival. He was a father to all who needed fathering. He wasn't one that would preach to people to the point of scaring them away, but he taught them what the Lord says about how to live a righteous life. By this I mean he always tried to guide and lead people in the right way, based on biblical principles. He used wisdom when giving direction and telling others about God, His goodness, and His promises. His job was to get people interested in learning about the Lord so that they would study on their own.

He made many mistakes and he wanted to show others how they could avoid the same pitfalls and go through the struggles. Sherrod learned how to quickly and honestly repent from wrongdoing. He would often tell others, "well, I know what the Lord has done for me and I can tell you about my experiences with Him." He learned that there is a better way to live life and he shared that way with all that would listen. He learned how to father from Buddy, his dad, and from his heavenly father.

"Big O" accepted Christ at an early age and united with Second Missionary Baptist Church under the leadership of Reverend Gilbert Jackson. As he matured in Christ and when Reverend Jackson left Second Baptist, Sherrod served faithfully (under the leadership of Reverend Albert Thomas) as a member of several auxiliaries: the Inspirational Choir, Bus and Young Progressive Adults Ministry, and the Deacon's Board.

He was employed at E.W. Bliss in Hastings, Michigan for several years. Orville was employed in the security department at a Battle Creek hospital for approximately 15 years from which he retired due to disability. In essence he lost his security job but he didn't lose his security because his security was in Christ Jesus. He did not let a physical disability hold him back from serving God. Sherrod's passion was God.

After retirement, he enjoyed serving as a Trustee, Deacon, and head of Church Security at a local church until death. While attending church, he was a member of the Usher Board, Prophetic, Compassion, and Life Experience Ministries. He also served as a leader for a Bible Study Cell Group.

He was a man that loved sports, (bowling, football, baseball) and his friends, but most of all he loved God. His hobbies were playing baseball, football, chess, and dominoes, bowling, and cooking for his friends and family. After several amputations, he was not able to bowl or play ball but he enjoyed watching sports and the cooking channels on television. His favorite sport was football and rightfully so. While in high school, he was a star football player. With his help, the Bearcats had a 20 game winning streak in 1966. His football team was one of the best in the State of Michigan. They scored 278 points while holding their opponents to 43 points. He represented the Bearcats on the all 6-A Team.

In 1979, "Big O" decided to make himself an honest man by asking for his sweetheart's hand in marriage. He asked her to marry him and to spend the rest of their lives together. He spent 26 good, bad, ugly, and indifferent years married to one woman . . . . Me. I was his first and only wife. He promised to love, honor, and respect the marriage vows until death, and he did. He knew how to be a husband and he knew how to be a friend. He spoiled me a little bit with his cooking, loving me, and celebrating my birthday with me the 31 days of March.

He was the king of his household and he ruled with love and kindness. He was an encourager and a peacemaker and I liked his wisdom and encouragement. He was a family man. He cooked and invited unexpected guests to dinner quite often. I'd come home on Sundays after church and he would tell me, "O by the way baby, _____ is coming over for dinner today. I cooked _____ and _____ and they will be here around 5:30." With a roll of the eyes and mumbling in my mouth I'd walk into the bedroom. I'd later come out and ask what he wanted me to do, knowing all the time that all he wanted me to do was sit and enjoy the meal, family, and friends. What a gracious host and cook. We enjoyed cookouts and great cuisine. Emriel was one of his favorite chefs and Sherrod used a lot of his recipes and spices.

Candlelight dinners were commonplace in our house. In fact, one time he had so many candles burning that I thought the house was on fire. He was a romantic. Bubble baths to candlelight and jazz was his way of helping me to relax from a long day at work. The house was always filled with fresh flowers because that was one his ways of showing his love for me. His grandmother did a good job of teaching him how to treat a woman.

He was one who didn't say much but when he made an impact on the lives of those that listened. When he spoke it was kind of like E.F. Hutton . . . everybody listened. He wasn't a stockbroker but he talked with many about Jesus so they could take stock in Him.

In fact, he invited the neighbors and others to church with him. He offered them rides to church. Often those he invited would say they didn't have suits to wear so they couldn't go to church. However, Sherrod reassured them that there are plenty of churches around that are interested in saving souls not in saving clothes. He told them that if they went to church and built a relationship with Christ, the clothes wouldn't matter.

He was "diligent to present himself approved of God, a worker who did not need to be ashamed, rightly dividing the word of truth" (II timothy 2:15, NKJV). He taught me a lot about God through our nightly Bible studies and through his actions. He was a man who loved Gospel music, jazz, sports, and cooking. He loved his friends, and his family. But most of all he loved Jesus Christ. He loved "the Lord his God with all his heart, with all his soul, with all his mind, and with all his strength Mark" (2:30, NKJV). When he was sick and required surgery, he trusted the doctors but most of all he trusted Jesus Christ as his healer. I remember when he went to have a fistula put in for dialysis. We checked in to the hospital at 7:00 A.M. and the doctors told us it would take 2-4 hours for the surgery. While he was in surgery, it seemed as though I was stuck in time. Everything stood still. Several hours passed. Everyone came and left the surgical waiting room. I remember there being a shift change and my godchild bringing me materials to read and food to eat. Then the doctor/surgeon came in to the waiting room. I saw the look on his face. It didn't look good. He said, "it was touch ad go but he's alright now." My response was "When I brought my husband in here he was alive and well, and all I want to hear from you is that he is alive and well." I was surprised when he looked at me and said, "Thanks be to God, he is all right." Sherrod died on the table but was resuscitated.

> You've met a lot of people from lots of places, and you've seen lots of faces . . . but let me introduce you to Him. Who is he?

Salt of the Earth . . . Light of the World
                                    Matthew 5:13-14

Abbreviations

AMP	Amplified Bible
KJV	King James Version
LASB	Life Application Study Bible
NKJV	New King James Version
NLT	New Living Translation
TLBP	The Living Bible Paraphrased

You Ought to Get to Know Him

You ought to get to know Him, this Mighty God that I serve. He's the King of the Universe. Yes, my God is Love. He's the only one who can keep you, keep you in perfect peace. He will help you fulfill your purpose, and then your soul He'll release to be free for eternity, no more pain and suffering. Take this from someone who knows, "You ought to get to know Him. I wanna tell you a story, about a mighty man of God, a man who was like a sailboat, powered by the tides, listening to the doctrines trying to find where to abide, met his Savior one day, when he was lost and confused. He allowed God to enter him, gave God his gifts to use. He showed others how to love God despite many ups and downs. He worshipped God through trials without complaint or a frown. And as his body grew weaker, each and every day, his faith grew ever stronger, and I can still hear him say, "You ought to get to know Him, this Mighty God that I serve. He's the King of the Universe. Yes, my God is Love. He's the only one who can keep you, keep you in perfect peace. He will help you fulfill your purpose and then your soul He'll release to be free for eternity, no more pain and suffering. Take this from someone who knows . . . You ought to get to know Him.

Remember that old sailboat once powered by the tides, was converted to a steam ship where God did abide. You know that a steam ship is powered from within. He was trying to tell everyone he met, strangers, friends, and kin, that there's a joy in serving Jesus, that's greater than the whole world holds. Despite your situation, you have got to be bold, when telling every, one you meet the greatest story ever told. You Ought to Get to Know Him, this Mighty God that I serve. He's the King of the Universe. Yes, my God is Love. He's the only one who can keep you, keep you in perfect peace. He will help you fulfill your purpose and then your soul He'll release to be free for eternity no more pain and suffering. Take this from someone who knows . . . You ought to get to know Him.

The lesson that he taught us, is one that I'll never forget. He showed us how to praise God wherever we are sent. He showed us how to worship in every circumstance. And I will share the good news each and every time, every time I get the chance. Since he's been freed from his body, his work is now ours to do. And you don't have to worry, I'll tell your son and my son, too . . . every time I get a chance, that we all have work to do . . . You Ought to Get to Know Him, this Mighty God that I serve. He's the King of the Universe. Yes, my God is Love. He's the only one who can keep you, keep you in perfect peace.

He will help you fulfill your purpose, and then your soul He'll release, to be free for eternity, no more pain and suffering. Take this from someone who knows you ought to get to know Him.

A MAN WHO WAS LIKE A SAILBOAT POWERED BY THE TIDES

Blessed is the man that endureth temptation: for when he is tried, he shall receive the crown of life, which the Lord hath promised to them that love him. Let no man say when he is tempted, I am tempted of God: for God cannot be tempted with evil neither tempteth he any man: But every man is tempted when he is drawn away of his own lust, and enticed (James 1:12-14, KJV).

Storms come in all our lives. Many times we feel equipped to weather the storms. We can run inside and hide in the shelter. But if we are young and trying to weather storms, we feel somewhat like a sailboat with a cloth sail being whipped by the winds on every side. There is no motor on the sailboat that can allow a quick escape from the elements. A sailboat has no motor. It is powered by tides of water that beat against the vessel and drives it on its way. The course is uncertain. Sometimes the tides are rough, other times calm. There is no way to predict which way the wind will blow the ship. However, each ship has a rudder so the ship can be turned wherever and whenever the pilot desires.

Unfortunately there are times when hurricanes, tornadoes, and Tsunamis come and with them come questions about whether or not the rudder will work when needed. When these storms come in our lives as adults we try to reason and understand what is happening. But when they come in the lives of children, they are confused and frightened. Sometimes the storms leave the child broken and lost. As a child of God, Sherrod was a ship in the midst of many storms. As a child, he often felt as though he was being tossed to and fro by his emotions.

When Sherrod's mother died, he was a young child. This was a tornado in his life. Her death left him devastated, broken, and motherless. That is when he got to know God as a mother to the motherless. His life had no real direction. At that time, he did not know that "He that dwelleth in the secret place of the most High shall abide under the shadow of the Almighty" (Psalm 91:1 KJV). Sure, he had his dad, sister, younger brother, and grandmother, but he lacked his mother's presence and guidance. His grandmother and dad raised him in the fear of the Lord. Because they believed that if they 'trained him in the way that he should go, so that when he was old he would not depart from it' (Proverbs 22:6, NKJV).

He attended the family church and listened to the pastor preach about the goodness of the Lord, but he felt lost, sad, confused, forgotten, and cheated out of time with his mother.

He often wondered where the Lord was when his mother died. All he knew was that one-day his mother went to the hospital and died. He blamed poor medical care and incompetent doctors for his mother's death. The aftermath of his mother's death left him lost and disconnected.

He needed more than anything to know that the Lord would "deliver him from the snare of the fowler, and from the noisome of pestilence." He desperately needed to be covered with God's feathers, so that under His wings he could trust because his trust was his only shield and buckler (Psalm 91:3-4, KJV). For this disconnection often showed up in his behavior and attitude towards others. His life was full of trials and tribulations, physical and emotional. He sought to understand the purpose of the pain. "For I know the plans I have for you," says the Lord. They are plans for good and not for evil, to give you a future and a hope" (Jeremiah 29:11 TLB).

In seeking answers he found "My brethren, count it all joy when ye fall into divers temptations; Knowing this, that the trying of your faith worketh patience. But let patience have her perfect work, that ye may be perfect and entire, wanting nothing. If any of you lack wisdom, let him ask God, that giveth to all men liberally, and upbraideth not; and it shall be given him. But let him ask in faith, nothing wavering.

For he that wavereth is like a wave of the sea driven with wind and tossed (James 1:2-6, KJV). He was disappointed in doctors and life. He had no joy. Being a child, he was not aware that the Bible says we can rejoice when we run into problems and trials, for we know that they are good for us—they help us learn to endure. And endurance develops strength of character in us, and character strengthens our confident expectation of salvation. He had to work out his own salvation with fear and trembling, for it is God who worked in him both to will and to do for His good pleasure (Philippians 2:13 NKJ).

The Lord sent him "help from the sanctuary, And strengthened him out of Zion" (Psalm 20:2). It was a blessing when one of Sherrod's male teachers took an interest in him and realized that if his anger were not redirected, he would become a casualty of society, a statistic. His teacher took him under his wings and got him involved in football. The Scripture tells us that "We then who are strong ought to bear with the scruples of the weak, and not to please ourselves.

Let each of us please his neighbor for his good, leading to edification. For even Christ did not please Himself; but as it is written, "The reproaches of those who reproached You fell on Me." For whatever things were written before were written for our learning, that we through the patience and comfort of the Scriptures might have hope. Now may the God of patience and comfort grant you to be like-minded toward one another, according to Christ Jesus, that you may with one mind and one mouth glorify the god and father of our Lord Jesus Christ. Therefore, receive one another, just as Christ also received us, to the glory of God (Romans 15:1-7 NKJV).

The Lord put it in Sherrod's football coach's heart to mentor him. There is an African proverb that says "It takes a village to raise a child." He realized that he was part of that village and in order for there to be unity and peace in the village; someone had to take on part of the responsibility of helping others to succeed. He knew that playing football was a more excellent way to take out aggression and anger. The steps of a good man are ordered by the Lord (Psalm 37:23 NKJV). So Sherrod became one of the best football players in the history of Battle Creek Central. The "God of hope filled Sherrod with all joy and peace in believing" in himself and in God, so that he abounded in hope by the power of the Holy Spirit (Romans 15:13).

As a football player, he was able to take out his anger, frustration, and disappointments in a constructive way on the Battle Creek Central football field. As a football player, he was one of 5 Junior Varsity grid men to represent Battle Creek Central High School in the 1966 all "6-A" State Champions team. Throughout the 1966 school year, he "played a vital part in key games." According to the 1966 Varsity Report, the varsity grid men rolled to a 6 win, 1 loss season record. Their lone defeat, which broke a twenty-two game winning streak spread over a four-year period, came at the hands of the East Lansing Trojans.

The season began with the Bearcats entertaining cross-town rival Lakeview, who they defeated quite handily, 31-6. After a slow start, the Bearcats offense began to roll in the second half. Kalamazoo and Lansing Sexton both fell, by scores of 36-7 and 39-19, respectively. At half time in the Sexton game, the score was 19-19, but Battle Creek completely dominated the rest of the game. Perhaps the highlight of the season was the Jackson game, held at C.W. Post Field. Held to a tie by Jackson the previous year, Battle Creek overwhelmed them, 38-0. Displaying a potent offense and a crushing defense, the Junior Varsity's garnered their fourth win in as many games.

Lansing Eastern was defeated in a driving rainstorm, 19-6. Battle Creek showed good poise under adverse weather conditions at many points during the encounter, the sign of a good team.

East Lansing was the next opponent of the Bearcats. On Trojan Field in East Lansing, the offense sputtered and the defense slipped as Battle Creek fell 29-14. The Junior Varsity's showed they were winners, however, with a 52-0 thrashing of Lansing Everett.

Bouncing back from their loss the previous week, nothing went wrong for Battle Creek as they finished their season on a winning note. Even though one streak was broken this year, another was continued for next year's team to add to. Since 1961, no Junior Varsity team at Battle Creek Central had lost a game at C.W. Post Field, certainly a remarkable record.

Sherrod's team added four more victories to this record. He knew what it meant to be a team player. He also knew what it meant to persevere. Playing football taught him a way to endure hardships with patience. Little did he know that football was building a foundation, preparing him for future hardships that would cause him to "pursue a godly life, along with faith, love, perseverance, and gentleness" (1 Timothy 6:11 LAB). Circumstances were created so that Sherrod could get to know Him personally.

LISTENING TO THE DOCTRINES TRYING TO FIND WHERE TO ABIDE

Abide in me, and I in you (St. John 15:4a NKJ).

Through running a football, he learned that he had to run in such a way that he would win. He was determined to be in the "Winners' Circle." Sherrod's success on the football field gave him what he needed to pursue a higher calling. That calling was in seeking God. He knew that if he wanted the eternal prize. He had to "Remember that in a race everyone runs but only one person gets the prize. He was determined to run in such a way that he would win. All athletes practice strict self-control. They do it to win a prize that will fade away, but Sherrod did it for an eternal prize" (I Corinthians 9:24-25).

So he became an active member of a Baptist church where he attended Sunday school, Bible classes, and served as a choir member, and a Deacon. Unfortunately, when he had a heart attach and the church members failed to visit and encourage him, he started studying with a friend from a different denomination at home. Having a desire and hunger for God, he listened to their doctrine trying to find where to abide.

After hearing many complaints from others, he discontinued his study with his friend and united with a nondenominational church where he met his Savior one-day and he no longer felt lost and confused. He allowed God to enter him, gave God his gifts to use. He continued studying and living the life he read about in the Bible. By visiting the sick and shut-in, taking the elderly to the store and to doctor appointments, getting up mornings at 5:00 a.m. praying for his pastor, family, friends, the neighborhood, country, state, and the world, he stepped into the ministry that God planned for him.

He had opportunities to "Declare his glory among the heathen, his wonders among the people, to say among the heathen that the Lord reigneth: the world also shall be established that it shall not be moved; he shall judge the people righteously (Psalm 96:3 & 10 NKJ). He mentored drug-addicts and fed the hungry. He encouraged others to accept Jesus as their personal savior and to join other believers. Our home was used for Bible study each week. He told others about the life that he lived before getting saved, and how much better his life had become because of accepting Jesus into his life. In doing so, he showed others how to love God despite many ups and downs.

Sherrod had 2 heart attacks, several amputations and surgeries: toes; feet; lower left leg; then the right leg above the knee; graphs; dialysis; MRSA; and he suffered temporary blindness.

He stepped on a nail while doing renovations at our house. He could not feel the nail cutting the bottom of his toe. When he discovered blood on his sock, he started trying to treat the cut himself. He was a diabetic and needed a doctor's care. He thought it was something that he could take care of. I insisted that he see a doctor. By the time he went to the doctor, the toe was gangrene and had to be amputated. This started a series of surgeries and hospital stays. Within a weeks time he had another toe amputated. After that healed, the remaining toes experienced trauma and had to be amputated. But he refused to let this stop Jesus' ministry through him. He giveth power to the faint; and to them that have no might he increaseth strength. Even the youths shall faint and be weary, and the young men shall utterly fall: But they that wait upon the Lord shall renew their strength; they shall mount up with wings as eagles; they shall run, and not be weary; and they shall walk, and not faint (Isaiah 40:29-31).

Sherrod grew accustomed to hospitals and trusted the employees to do what they were trained to do. Unfortunately, I too, believed that nurses were angels of mercy and that most doctors were ethical. We had no reason to believe otherwise. After all, his experiences so far were good. While in the hospital, he continued witnessing to everyone that came into his room. After the second above the knee amputation, he fell out of the hospital bed and lay on the floor for half an hour. His roommate said nurses and aides kept passing by the room but never stopped in to help. While talking with his roommate, I found out everything that had happened. Sherrod did not want me to make a big deal out of it. He still had confidence in the staff and in the hospital. I told him he must have made some enemies while working there because he was invisible to them. I waited for the nurse to come in to tell me about his fall but she didn't. So I called her in to ask what happened. Her response was that she was going to tell me about it but she just hadn't gotten around to it. Sherrod had called the nurses earlier before he fell out of the bed but there was a great delay in their coming to see about him. After he fell, his roommate called them but there was still a delay.

I was concerned that they did not know his name but they knew his roommates' name. His roommate had his name and his nurses' name posted on the board above his bed. Sherrod didn't. I started questioning their methods: opening needle caps with their mouth; dropping needle caps and used band aids on the floor and leaving them there; and washing the eating table with the same rag that they used to wash the sinks, windowsills and chairs.

I was concerned about him maintaining his dignity while in the hospital. When he was taken to dialysis while in the hospital, he was left uncovered and lying in feces for a long period of time. What happened to the angels of mercy? Another concern was that Sherrod had specific instructions written above his bed not to take vitals in the arm with the fistula. Those that came in to take his blood pressure did not read the sign and attempted to do so but I was there to stop them. I had to remind them about the sign and his life line. They responded with anger and indifference. They also forgot to feed him that day. When I asked them for food, they said the kitchen was closed but they could give him some applesauce. I called some friends and they brought up food for him.

He worshipped God through trials without a complaint or a frown. He came to understand what so few ever learn (Philippians 1:29, NKJ). He now understood what it meant when the Bible says He will feed the hungry. Additionally, he learned how God supplies our every need. When the hospital wouldn't feed him, friends came to the rescue. He learned that Jesus is the Divine Physician because even though he was mistreated, he never held a grudge. According to Philippians 1:29 (NKJV), "suffering is a gift from God, for in the midst of suffering He comforts us and enables us to rejoice." I Peter says that suffering is a blessing because it brings eternal reward. Hebrews 2:10 and James 1:2-4 assure us that God sees suffering as a tool to accomplish His purposes both in His son and in His children. Suffering causes us to become mature Christians.

A sound heart is life to the body (Proverb 14:30a NKJV). As his body grew weaker each and every day, his faith grew ever stronger, and I can still hear him say, "You ought to get to know Him, this mighty

God that I serve. Sherrod did not allow pain, disappointment, neglect, or abuse separate him from the Lord and his faith in God. He is the King of the Universe. Yes, my God is Love. He is the only one, who can keep you in perfect peace. He will help you fulfill your purpose, and then your soul He will release to be free for eternity, no more pain and suffering.

Take this from someone who knows, you ought to get to know Him. "Who then can ever keep Christ's love from us? When we have trouble or calamity, when we are hunted down or destroyed, is it because he doesn't love us anymore?

And if we are hungry, or penniless, or in danger, or threatened with death, has God deserted us? No, for the Scriptures tell us that for his sake we must be ready to face death at every moment of the day—we are like sheep awaiting slaughter; but despite all this, overwhelming victory is ours through Christ who loved us enough to die for us. For I am convinced that nothing can ever separate us from his love. Death can't, and life can't. The angels won't, and all the powers of hell itself cannot keep God's love away. Our fears for today, our worries about tomorrow, or where we are—high above the sky, or in the deepest ocean—nothing will ever be able to separate us from the love of God demonstrated by our Lord Jesus Christ when he died for us" (Romans 8: 35-39 TLBP).

HE SHOWED OTHERS HOW TO PRAISE GOD

I will praise You, O Lord, with my whole heart; I will tell of all Your marvelous works. I will be glad and rejoice in You; I will sing praise to Your name, O Most High" (Psalm 9:1-2 NKJV).

If there is one thing that Sherrod loved, it was praising the Lord. He wasn't ashamed to throw his hands in the air and shout Hallelujah! It was even more exciting to see him raise his arms above his head in total adoration of his God. I love hearing him shout out "Thank You Jesus for all you did for me when you died on the cross!" He knew that everything he needed was already done on the cross. He was not ashamed to open his mouth and praise the Lord. He believed God's promises to him and His promises for his family. Sherrod made it perfectly clear to all those around him that his little light was going to shine for Jesus in all that he did. Some thought he was foolish because they couldn't see what the Lord had done for him. None the less, he and the Lord knew how much Sherrod had gone through and how much more was in store for him to endure.

He took every opportunity to celebrate his God. Before Sherrod became a new creation in Christ, he was quiet and reserved.

Afterwards, he shouted like a warrior who had just won a great battle. When he shouted Glory! It echoed throughout the building. He was proud to be a Christian. His Baptist upbringing went right out the spiritual window. It was amazing what he could do with one leg. I remember when he fell to his knees/knee, lifted his hands, and just blessed the lord. Afterwards, he got up without hesitation and walked calmly to his seat. Oh what a day. He didn't ask God for anything. He just blessed God's name. He expressed his adoration for having God was in his life. The expression on his face made me feel like Sherrod had actually touched the hem of Hid garment. Even though Sherrod didn't sing, knew how to make a joyful noise. So in his own way, under the power of the Holy Spirit, he sang and used his voice as an instrument for God. He learned how to rejoice in all things and situations. God inhabits the praises of His people (Psalm 22:3 KJV).

My mother use to sing a song: "Every Christian ought to stand up and testify. And say for the Lord I'll live and for the Lord I'll die. You may not be able to sing like angels. You may not be able to preach like Paul. But you can say I love the Lord and He heard my cry. And then he died to save us all. I want the whole world to know that I know a man and if I couldn't say a word, I'd raise my hands. And if you've got it, I mean that ole time religion, you ought to show some sign."

Well, Sherrod could not sing or preach but he certainly enjoyed raising his hands, shouting hallelujah, and praising the Lord. His fervent prayers and praise started after the first heart attack and two toe amputations. Sherrod was grateful for what God and others did for him and he demonstrated it in his high praise. He was just thankful to be alive. He couldn't wait to get to Church. Before returning to church, he had phantom pains. He often said it felt like his toes were itching.

Not too long after the two toes were amputated, his foot was amputated. The pain was excruciating. The pain made it almost impossible for him to sleep. In spite of the sleepless nights, he had so much faith in God that when he stayed up all night, he still got dressed to go to church. He believed that his victory over pain was in his praise. When the Holy Spirit came upon Sherrod, the phantom pain and the itch stopped. He used to say that he knew he didn't have his foot but it felt like it. When Sherrod praised God, he was sincere and he got results. He demonstrated his appreciation to God with his praise. He did not want to miss an opportunity to praise God. With the first amputation, Sherrod was fitted for prosthesis.

After weeks and weeks of treatments and therapy, he learned to walk again. Even though he had prosthesis, no one knew because he had no limp. It was quite a sight to see my husband walking around the church with his hands raised and singing God's praises. He wasn't the best singer in the world but he sure knew how to make a joyful noise. I remember the time our oldest granddaughter and daughter came to the church and my granddaughter saw her grandfather singing in the choir stand. She looked at me and said, "Look at papa. He's singing but he doesn't know the words. He sings loud on the parts he knows and moves his mouth on the other parts." My daughter threatened to separate us because we were laughing and talking in church. Imani couldn't figure out why her papa was in a choir.

It sure made me proud to know that my husband was saved. I enjoyed seeing and hearing him say Hallelujah and speak in tongues. To hear him say thank you Jesus was like music to my ears. When he said praise the Lord, chills went down my spine. Oh what a feeling. I remember thinking to God be the Glory. I'd never seen Sherrod so expressive. Ordinarily he was quiet and reserved. So to hear him shout out hallelujah stirred many emotions. I'd never heard him shout Hallelujah so loudly. The first time I ever saw him fall down and worship God made me the proudest woman alive. At that moment, I knew what it felt like to be in heaven. It was great to see this change in my husband.

It made me prouder than ever to be his wife. I knew that from that day forward our life would never be the same. Something miraculous had happened.

REMEMBER THAT OLD SAILBOAT ONCE POWERED BY THE TIDES

The mighty oceans have roared, O Lord. The mighty oceans roar like thunder; the mighty oceans roar as they pound the shore. But the mightier of the violent raging seas, mightier than the breakers of the shore—the Lord above is mightier than these! (Psalm 93:3-4, LASB).

This book affords one an opportunity to remember why Sherrod lived, and believed in Jesus Christ, and what he stood for. Psalm 93:3-4 let's us know that trouble, sickness, and disappoints will come but we can endure all things when we have a relationship with Jesus Christ. A relationship with Jesus Christ will change you from a sailboat to a steam ship. Sherrod started out as a sailboat. He underwent many trials and tribulations. Sherrod had 2 heart attacks, several amputations, graphs, dialysis, Mercer, and he suffered temporary blindness. This was his Tsunami. The body that he once had was gone. His way of life was gone but he did not lose heart.

Paul writes in Ephesians 4:13-19, therefore I ask that you do lose heart at my tribulations for you, which is your glory. For this reason I bow my knees to the father of our Lord Jesus Christ, from whom the whole family in heaven and earth is named, that He would grant you, according to the riches of His glory, to be strengthened with might through His Spirit in the inner man, that Christ may dwell in your hearts through faith; that you being rooted and grounded in love, may be able to comprehend with all the saints what is the width and length and depth and height to know the love of Christ which passes knowledge; that you may be filled with all the fullness of God." He knew that "Those who live in the shelter of the Most High will find rest in the shadow of the Almighty" (Psalm 91:1 LASB).

After this realization, he was converted to a steam ship where God did abide. John 15:4 says, "abide in me, and I in you. As the branch cannot bear fruit of itself, except it abide in the vine; no more can ye, except ye abide in me." Jesus is the vine and Sherrod knew he was the branch. Therefore, he found his abode in Jesus and Jesus in him brought forth fruit, because without Jesus, Sherrod realized he could do nothing. With Jesus in him, Sherrod meditated on Jesus' words day and night. Jesus' words were with him and in him.

This being the case, Sherrod knew that he could "ask what he would, and it would be done (St. John 15:7, NKJ). Now he had power and was transformed by the renewing of his mind. He became a steamship.

You know that a steam ship is powered from within. The Holy Spirit became his guide and he started telling everyone he met, strangers, friends and kin, that there's a joy in serving Jesus, that's greater than the whole world holds. He lived 'goodness, filled with knowledge, and was able to admonish others' (Romans 15:14). He let everyone he talked to know that despite their situation, they have to be bold when telling every one they meet the greatest story ever told . . . . the Jesus story. You ought to get to know Him this Mighty God that he served. He's the King of the Universe. Yes, God is Love. He's the only one who can keep you in perfect peace.

HE'LL KEEP YOU IN PERFECT PEACE

Isaiah 26:3-4, (NKJ) Thou wilt keep him in perfect peace, whose mind is stayed on thee: because he trusteth in thee.

Trust ye in the Lord forever for in the Lord Jehovah is everlasting strength. He is the only one who can keep you in perfect peace (I Peter 5:10-11, NJKV) But may the God of all grace, who called us to His eternal glory by Christ Jesus, after you have suffered a while, perfect, establish, strengthen, and settle you. To Him be the glory and the dominion forever and ever. Amen.

Sherrod refused to give up in times of struggle. He had a peace that was beyond my understanding. When he had one toe amputated, I asked him why he didn't just have the whole foot amputated because of poor circulation. He said if the doctor could save the foot, he was going to give him an opportunity to do so. He believed his part in the whole matter was to listen to the doctors. He had the surgery the surgery and it was successful but he later got gangrene and the doctors had to do a below the knee amputation. After he was released, I irrigated the wound twice daily, he healed and was fitted for prosthesis. He did his part with therapy and learned to walk again.

He did well for several years. Then he developed a sore and gangrene on the other foot and had another below the knee amputation that did not heal. We tried wound vacuums and debridding but his flesh started falling from the bone and he had to go back into the hospital for more surgery. He trusted the surgeon when he released him from the hospital to go to a nursing home. The surgeon said the nursing home was one of the best in the city and that he was only going there because he'd get better care. Unfortunately, this was not the case. He pretty much had to do everything for himself even though he was told not to get out of the bed without help. I stayed with him to help out until around 11:30 each night and I went to visit on my lunch breaks and after work to make sure he received proper care. When I got to there, he said it had been over an hour since he rang his buzzer for help. I went to the nurses' station and asked who his nurse was. The two people at the nurses' station ignored me. I asked again and the nurse asked, "Who wants to know?" I told her who I was and asked if she could help Sherrod to the restroom. She said she would when she was done passing out medication, which would be at least a couple of hours.

I asked who her supervisor was and what time she'd be in the next day because I wanted to have a meeting with her about the quality of care given there. During the meeting, Sherrod remained calm. The supervisor apologized and said she'd take care of the problem because she had several complaints about this nurse. I asked for either Sherrod's release or the nurses' release. Because of the peace that God gave him, he never got upset or faltered in his beliefs.

Orville believed that we all play a part in choosing life or death. After all, he had already gone through several storms, loss of toes and feet. He knew that having one toe, one leg, even two legs amputated wasn't the end for him. He believed that God worked through the doctors. His trust was in God, not in man. He said whatever God had for him was for him. He had confidence in the doctor's ability, but most of all, he trusted in Jesus. He said "baby, this time it's different. He was trying to prepare me for his death. In fact, he asked me "do you think the Lord is ready for me now?" I just kept saying, "Not now. Just get well and come home." I wasn't ready for him to die. It is a given that our health will fade and we will die. Job said "How frail is man, how few his days, how full of trouble! He blossoms for a moment like a flower-and withers; as the shadow of a passing cloud, he quickly disappears" (Job 14:1-2, LBP). Our days are numbered and we have but a little while to do God's will. Sherrod believed that we all should be about our father's business . . . . Evangelizing and praising God so that He can get the glory out of our lives. Therefore, he lived each day like it was his last. Everywhere he went, he found an opportunity to proclaim the Good News.

The Word of the Lord tried him. Regardless to what came his way, sickness, health, weakness, pain, amputations, he was a Christian and he did not want to let God down. He believed that God still had something for him to do. He had a job, a responsibility, not only to himself, but to all the people that he touched every day. And so, one person does make a difference. He made a difference in the lives of others by demonstrating his trust and faith in God and His promises. In spite of all the suffering he endured, he learned to commit to God so that he could reign with Him. He was passionate about fulfilling his purpose and assignment through the suffering.

He took seriously his responsibility as a husband and head of his household. He was my husband, the priest, pastor and king of his household and he treated me like his "good thing, his queen." He who finds a wife finds a good thing, and obtains favor from the Lord (Proverbs 18:22, NKJV).

Husbands love your wives just as Christ also loved the church and gave Himself for her, that he may sanctify and cleanse her with the washing of water by the word, that He might present her to Himself a glorious church, not having spot or wrinkle or any such thing, but that she should be holy and without blemish. So husbands ought to love their own wives as their own bodies; he who loves his wife loves himself. For no one ever hated his own flesh, but nourishes and cherishes it, just as the Lord does the church. For we are members of His body, of His flesh and of His bones.

For this reason a man shall leave father and mother and be joined to his wife, sand the two shall become one flesh (Ephesians 5:25-31, NKJV). We became one flesh and I was his "good thing."

Consequently, my life plan has taken loops and turns that I never imagined, expected or wanted. Sherrod dying before me was not part of my plan. When we said 'til death do us part," I never imagined Sherrod would die before me. In fact, I never thought about him dying because he was so full of life. After all, he had two heart attacks and didn't die. He was my superman, my hero. Although I know it is appointed unto man to die, I did not expect death to come so soon. It seemed that our life was just beginning and then he died. I still find it hard to believe. Many days it doesn't seem real. I drive up in my driveway and expect to smell the aroma of food coming out of his kitchen.

I walk in the house and expect to hear him say, "Baby, is that you? How was your day? Tell me everything." I still expect to hear him scurrying around in an attempt to turn off the television before I get to the bedroom where he was. I still expect to see the table set with fresh flowers and a special dish that he'd prepared with a recipe from the cooking channel. Sometimes it just doesn't seem real. When I walk into the bedroom I can sometimes smell the fragrance of his cologne. When I work in the yard I am reminded of the times we'd disagree about doing the edging and the direction in which the grass should be cut. When I drive in the car and it's dirty, I am reminded of the times when he'd take the car and work on cleaning and polishing it to perfection. Even the air vents were dust-free when he detailed it. The tires looked new and the interior had that new car smell. He was very meticulous and conscientious. There are still times that I ask God why the good die young. But the answer is always the same, "the length of our lives is as uncertain as the morning fog—now you see it; soon it is gone" (James 4:14b TLBP).

He taught me a lot about God through his behavior and his actions. He was one who didn't talk a lot but when he talked he impacted my life and the lives of others. He loved people and those who knew him reciprocated the love.

When he was with others, he made them feel like they were the only people in the room. The way he treated people made them feel like they were the most important people in the world. He just had a way about him that made others happy just to be in his presence.

His demeanor was somewhat priestly. He knew how to take charge and lead without being harsh. Getting to know God made all the difference in his life. For he had truly become a new creation in Christ. Therefore, if any is in Christ, he is a new creation; old things have passed away, behold, all things have become new II Corinthians 5:17, NKJV). He knew that he was a royal priesthood and that he was the righteousness of God. So as a saved man, a new creature, a priest, his only choice was to strive to please God. He did not want to do anything that would cause him to lose favor with God. He became the Lord's prisoner and liked it. He learned to "walk worthy of the vocation wherewith he was called" (Ephesians 4:1 KJV).

He did all he could to help others get to know God through him. For example, when he invited people to church, he provided transportation for them to get there. His joy was in helping others. Although he could not help as many as he wanted, he helped all he could. Before Sherrod gave his heart and life to Christ, he was blind spiritually. He wasn't anxious to help others. He never refused to help others if they asked for help. But after he became the new man in Christ, he looked for opportunities to help others. I think that after he lost his physical sight due to diabetes, he was more determined than ever to do something, anything to help others. He had a heart for people and he never grew weary in well doing. Sherrod loved people and he loved doing things for others.

No matter how sick the doctors told him he was, he believed God's report, "My son, attend to my words, incline thine ear unto my sayings. Let them not depart from thine eyes; keep them in the midst of thine heart. For they are life unto those that find them, and health to all their flesh (Proverbs 4:20-22 KJV).

Although he went to dialysis three days per week, he stayed strong enough to drive himself there and back. Others in his dialysis group were so weak that they had to be transported. Some days he'd go to dialysis and while there talking with other patients, one of them would die during dialysis. But the Lord kept him strong. He did not sorrow, "for the joy of the Lord was his strength" (Nehemiah 8:10 NKJV). It was the strength of the Lord enabled him to leave dialysis and go out and do something good for others. He seemed to never grow weary of well doing.

The Bible says in Galatians 6:9 & 10, "And let us not grow weary while doing good, for in due season we shall reap if we do not lose heart." Therefore, as we have opportunity, let us do good to and for all, especially to those who are of the household of faith. We should all strive to do as Sherrod did; he helped others and seemed to never grow tired of doing good deeds. He gave his brother rides to work when he had no transportation. He took the elderly shopping for groceries and ran errands for them. He provided transportation to others that needed rides to church. He cooked and took food to the bereaved. He was a member of the Compassion Ministry at his church and he visited the sick and shut-in.

He showed his love for God by rendering service to people. He was available to be used by God. One day when I came home from work he was sitting in his car waiting. He said, "Baby you can't go in the house yet. He proceeded to tell me about an older gentleman that he met earlier that day at a local store. The man was on a walker and was walking extremely slow across the parking lot and Sherrod thought he was going to get hit by a car. He was having some difficulties getting around so he offered to help. He asked him where he was going and offered him a ride home.

He man accepted the ride, and on the way to his house, Sherrod found out the man was a retired minister who had been living with his daughter in an apartment building nearby. Unfortunately, the daughter had relocated and abandoned the man and his wife in the apartment. They kept the apartment when she left.

Sherrod took him home. But when they arrived, he discovered the man had decayed food on the stove and in the refrigerator. He went to the store and spent his last penny to buy food for that man and his wife. When I came home from work that evening, he was sitting in his car on the street, waiting. He said, "Baby you can't go in the house yet. You have to help me." I thought something was wrong with him but there wasn't. He said there is a family that needs help. I have to help them." I thought sure, I'm the one that is going to have to help because what can Sherrod possible do to help? Being the obedient, loving, wife, I listened and we took action. We went to see the couple to find out if they would accept our help.

When we got there, we saw that the house was infested with mice and there were mouse droppings all over the kitchen table and floor. There was a cat in the house and a nasty litter box. The man's wife was upstairs, in bed and she couldn't walk. There was a port-a-potty at the foot of the bed but it was full of feces. The wife lay in bed on a mattress that was soaked through with urine. There was no covering on the matters and the urine had soaked through to the carpet on the floor. In the upstairs bathroom, there was a toilet full of feces and the smell in the room was sickening. Sherrod and I carried 5-gallon buckets of water from our house to theirs to flush the toilet. We solicited help from my church to get the house cleaned up and to get emergency assistance for the family. And because of Sherrod, the minister and his wife now live in a better place. And they have food and shelter that is affordable for them. He put the needs of others ahead of his.

During his blindness, he learned that Jesus was his healer, he regained his sight. But during the blindness he continued helping others by encouraging them over the phone. Sherrod was able to heal the broken hearted with his encouraging words. After regaining his sight, he made a point to visit and help his aunts and uncles, his grandmother, stepmother, and single mothers. He had a pastor's heart. He cared about people and he wanted them to be saved. He never gave up on people and he never gave up his belief that in order to live a good life, one must be saved. He was my pastor. He was the kind of man that wouldn't go to bed without reading what he called "his word." He taught me to read the word to him and with him. When I sat with him at the hospital he'd ask, "Where's my word?" Sherrod insisted that we read the Bible together each night when we went to bed. We had to lie down and wake up with the Word of God. One of the most pleasurable memories in our marriage for me was when he went blind. He said that he couldn't see the word but he wanted me to read to him. Even though he could not see how to read the Bible, he had memorized Scripture so that when he couldn't see it he could quote it. So, every day and night we spent time together getting to know God and each other through the Word of God. In spite of the blindness, we both knew his blindness was temporary.

Therefore, I had him make me a promise that when he regained his sight, he would read to me. Surgery was immanent because blood vessels had burst in his eyes. He got his sight back after surgeons removed blood from the back of his eyes, and he kept that promise. Each night we took turns reading to each other. Listening to him read to me each night helped me fall asleep. I enjoyed falling asleep in his arms and in the arms of God. I felt safe and secure in his arms. After I'd fall asleep, he'd get up, go into the office and pray. Some nights I'd wake up, peek into the office and see him rubbing his hands and thighs, praying and crying out to God for others.

He kept me on track. When I spread myself too thin, he had a way of always bringing me back to reality by helping me to realize how much I could physically and emotionally handle.

I remember when I was working and going to school full time. I was stressed out and ready to give up and quit school. He asked me, "Verda, how would that be beneficial? Who would it help? You are not a quitter. So what are you going to do? What do you think would happen if you just studied one subject at a time and complete the work for that and then move on to the next?" I thought about it and realized that he was right. Having done that, I am continuing my education. He was a wise encourager and he often said my accomplishments were his accomplishments. He was proud of many of the things that I did in the home, in school, in church, and in the community.

I laugh now at some of the things he said to me because I think he wanted me to continue my education so that he could have some peace at home when he was watching television. I use to complain about him watching television when I got home. But I had a friend who also had a heart attack and she told me that many times she had her television on to quiet the silence and as background noise. When one is laid up in bed, what else do they have? I realized that Sherrod watched Christian television mostly. That's where he got his strength to go on. So I stopped nagging and complaining. In fact, I started watching television with him (sometimes). He shared the TV evangelists' messages with me.

He seemed to never grow weary of well doing even on his worse days. There were times when Sherrod was too weak to walk down the ramp to get to his car to drive to dialysis. He fell down many times and was unable to get up on his own. Fortunately, Jesus sent neighbors to pick him up and either help him to the car or into the house, to God be the glory. When he fell in a parking lot, many people let him lie on the ice because they didn't want to get involved. However, God sent a trucker by a street that ordinarily does not get large trucks. The driver saw Sherrod, stopped, and helped him get to home. He later went to the hospital for surgery because he had a fractured knee. God's angels had charge over Sherrod and kept him in all his ways. The angels bore him up in their hands because God set his love upon him, therefore He delivered him: He was with him in trouble; He delivered him, and honoured him (Psalm 91:11-16). The knee healed quickly. "He cried unto the Lord and He healed him (Psalm 30:2). After the knee healed, he fell again in the hallway of our home, I was there. Again, he had to have surgery on his knee. He never complained. All he said was, "Verda, it could be worse."

"Many are the afflictions of the righteous: but the Lord delivereth him out of them all (Psalm 34:19). Through it all he learned to trust in Jesus. He had perfect peace. After healing from surgery, he went back to evangelizing and helping others.

He said he had to work while he still had time. His only choice was to share the good news every time he got chance. It was important for him to tell your son and his son, too that we all have work to do. He wanted all to know that God is the King of the universe and our God is Love. He wanted everyone to know that God is the only one who can keep you in perfect peace. Sherrod was not ashamed to tell people that "God will help you fulfill your purpose and then your soul He'll release to be free for eternity. And when your work on earth is done, there will be no more pain and suffering. Once you get to know him, all trials and tribulations will be over. There will be no more storms. You'll no longer be tossed and driven, battered and scorned, and there will be life everlasting with Jesus Christ." Sherrod worked hard to win souls for Christ. Now it is your turn.

Jeremiah 1:5 & 11(KJV) "Before I formed thee in the belly I knew thee; and before thou camest forth out of the womb I sanctified thee, and I ordained thee a prophet unto the nations.

For I know the thoughts that I think towards you, saith the Lord, thoughts of peace, and not evil, to give you an expected end." Sherrod finished the assignment that God had for him and Jesus was with him all the way. He maintained hope throughout his assignment. He fought a good fight. He ran a good race and then his soul was released to be free for eternity; no more pain and suffering. God saw him through his assignment to a glorious conclusion.

"For I know the plans I have for you," declares the Lord, "plans to prosper you and not to harm you, plans to give you hope and a future" (Jeremiah 29:11 NIV). So here I am, living in a plan that is not of my doing. Yes even the best laid plans go amuck when the plans are not God's plans. The plan looks nothing like I ever could have imagined. For example, I never imagined, expected, or wanted to be a widower. This just shows how "We can make our plans, but the final outcome is in God's hands" (Proverbs 16:1 TLB).

Before he died, he looked up toward heaven and smiled. As I talked to him, he never stopped looking up. He answered my questions and responded to what I said. But he would not look at me. He was looking at something that I could not see. It was then that the nurse asked him if he wanted some pain medication but he seemed not to hear her. So I repeated the question. He looked at me and said "for what? I feel no pain." His final words to me were, "baby, tell them, they ought to get to know Him. I asked who? And with a glow on his face, he looked up towards heaven and said, "God".

Sherrod died as he lived, surrounded by friends and family. Wherefore seeing we also are compassed about with so great a cloud of witnesses, let us lay aside every weight and the sin which doth so easily beset us, and let us run with patience the race that is set before us. Looking unto Jesus the author and finisher of our faith; who for the joy that was set before him endured the cross, despising the shame, and set down at the right hand of the throne of God (Hebrews 12:1-2, KJV). Take this from someone who knows . . . You ought to get to know Him.

THE LESSON THAT
HE TAUGHT US

"Blessed is the man who trusts in the Lord And whose hope is the Lord. For he shall be like a tree planted by the waters, Which spreads out its roots by the river, and will not fear when heat comes; But its leaf will be green, And will not be anxious in the year of drought, Nor will cease from yielding fruit" (Jeremiah 17:7-8, NKJV).

Sherrod studied and meditated on God's word day and night. Even then he did not know everything there is to know about God. No one knows everything there is to know about God but according to Psalm 139:1-6, He knows everything about us: "O LORD, you have searched me and you know me. You know when I sit and when I rise; you perceive my thoughts from afar. You discern my going out and my lying down; you are familiar with all my ways. Before a word is on my tongue you know it completely, O LORD. You hem me in—behind and before; you have laid your hand upon me. Such knowledge is too wonderful for me, too lofty for me to attain."

He was hungry for the Word of God. That's why he studied. The more he learned about God, the more he wanted to share it with others. As such he taught us all a lesson worth learning. The lesson that he taught us is one that I'll never ever forget. He showed us how to praise God wherever we are sent. "Wherefore, my beloved, as ye have always obeyed, not as in my presence only, but now much more in my absence, work out your own salvation with fear and trembling" (Philippians 2:12 KJV).

He had a heart attack when we were in the mall in Chicago and Mall Security paged me over the intercom. Sherrod refused to go to the hospital in Chicago so he drove back to Battle Creek, and went to bed. When the pain became unbearable, I took him to the local hospital, where they flew him to Kalamazoo for surgery. I believe it was at that time that Jesus did spiritual surgery on his heart. I believe this because he had no fear and he remained calm when they told him he needed heart surgery. He never showed fear for 'God did not give him the spirit of fear; but of power, and of power, and of love, and of a sound mind' (II Timothy 1:7 KJV).

After surgery, he witnessed to the nurses, doctors and all that came to visit him. Sherrod "cried unto the Lord with his voice, and the Lord heard him out of his holy hill. He laid down and slept; awaked; for the Lord sustained him (Psalms 3:4-5 KJV).

He showed us how to worship in every circumstance, death of his father, disappointment in relatives, and amputations. He "gave unto the Lord the glory due to His name; worshipped the Lord in the beauty of holiness (Psalms 29:2.)" He praised God in the midst of his pain and suffering because he trusted Jesus as his Divine Physician (Mark 2:17).

Sherrod had complete confidence in Jesus to heal him. He told me that even if Jesus didn't heal him he knew he could. He never thought he'd escape this world without pain. Through it all he remained calm and had unshakable faith for he knew "A calm and undisturbed mind and heart are the life and health of the body (Proverb 14:30a AMP). He praised Him when he went blind because he knew that "The Lord openeth the eyes of the blind: the Lord raiseth them that are bowed down: the Lord loveth the righteous (Psalm 146:8 KJV). In the midst of the praise, God sent increase in health and finances. Friends would stop by to give him money. But when he received the money, he used it to help others. "For the needy shall not always be forgotten: the expectation of the poor shall not perish forever (Psalms 9:18, KJV). Sherrod was "an example to all believers in what he taught, in the way he lived, in his love, in his faith, and his purity (I Timothy 4:12b LASB).

He never stopped praising God for his goodness and mercy. He knew he was a sinner saved by grace. He was excited about his new life in Christ and he demonstrated this wherever he went, especially in church. It was exciting to see a one legged man run around the church with his hands lifted up and his mouth filled with praise. On lookers wondered what he had to praise God so hard. During his long illness, close friends and family asked "where is your God now? Where is your God when you need him?" His answer to them was "even if God chooses not to heal me, He will be glorified because I know that He can. I know my redeemer lives." He put his trust in God and not in man. Heal me, O Lord, and I shall be healed; Save me, and I shall be saved, For You are my praise. Indeed they say to me, Where is the word of the Lord? Let it come now! As for me, I have not hurried away from being a shepherd who follows You, Nor have I desired the woeful day; You know what came out of my lips; It was right there before You. Do not be a terror to me; You are my hope in the day of doom.

Let them be ashamed who persecute me, But do not let me be put to shame; Let them be dismayed, But do let me be dismayed. Bring on them the day of doom, And destroy them with double destruction!

(Jeremiah 17:14-18, NKJV). Sherrod often said he was created to praise God because he believed and was determined to "praise the name of the Lord: for He commanded, and he was created.

He also stablished him forever and ever: He made a decree which did not pass (Psalm 148:5 & 6.)" Because of his praise, he was delivered from the snare of death. He came through the first heart surgery with flying colors. The Bible says "Let everything that has breath praise the Lord (Psalm 150:6KJV), and he obeyed.

Unfortunately, he stepped on a nail, got gangrene and had one of his little toes amputated. Within the same week, he had another toe amputated. He did not get depressed. Instead, he said "I still have 8 toes left." Because the circulation in his foot was bad, there was yet another amputation. After that amputation, there was a vein graph to increase circulation to the foot. This surgery was unsuccessful, leading to amputation of the foot. Still, he was liberal in his praise because he knew that his blessing was in the praise. He wanted God to get the glory out of his life.

Just as God delivered Israel because of her praise, Sherrod knew that God would deliver him. So he "cried unto the Lord and was delivered: he trusted in God, and was confounded Psalm 22:5, KJV). He came home from the hospital and I irrigated the wound and nursed him through this trying period. During this time he quoted Psalms 27:7, 9, and 11a, "Hear, O Lord, when I cry with my voice; have mercy also upon me, and answer me. Hide not thy face far from me; put not thy servant away in anger: thou hast been my help; leave me not, neither forsake me, O God of my salvation. Teach me thy way, O Lord, and lead me in a plain path," and I will share the good news each and every time I get the chance.

As I Lay in My Hospital Bed

He heals the brokenhearted and binds their wounds
(Psalm 147:3).

As I lay in my bed, I thought about my daughter, Tisha, whom I love so very much. My thoughts were of her loving words and her soft, gentle touch. I thought about her kindness and the gift of love she so willingly gave throughout the years. And these thoughts made it hard to hold back the tears. Her presence in my life helped to fill the void and I know within my heart that she is truly a gift from God.

As I lay in my hospital bed, many thoughts went through my head. I wondered what my son's life would be like for he had just begun. I wondered about his life's journey because he is my only son. I wondered where he was as I called out his name. I knew that after today his life would never be the same. When Verda said he was coming to see me I said, "he's too busy". She said "don't talk like that it only makes me crazy." She reassured me of your love for me because your love I could not see, because there were so many times that I longed for you to be with me.

I think about my granddaughters who brightened up my life. My first granddaughter, Imani, I would not trade her for any amount of money. She is my first granddaughter, but by far not my last. Those great big eyes that sparkle bright let me know that no matter what happens, everything is already all right. Then there is Zea'Mya, the second apple of my eye. When I pretend to fall asleep in my chair, she hides my prosthesis and when I wake, I pretend to cry. She hides behind the chair and asks if I can find her there. The thoughts of my grandchildren help me through this strife. I hope they will remember me when I'm no longer there to cook, but perhaps as they read my words they will appreciate this book. For on each page is written words of how they brought me joy and how late at night when they were not aware, I kept them in my heart and in every word of my prayers.

I thought about my sister, dad, grandmother, and my mother. And many times I thought about my brother. When I thought about my sister, I longed to see her face and hear her voice, but as I lay in my bed I realized that to see me again would definitely be her choice.

When I thought about my dad, it made me glad because I knew that soon I would see him face to face because alas I have come to the end of this old race. "I have fought a good fight, I have finished the race, and I have remained faithful. And now the prize awaits—the crown of righteousness that the Lord, the righteous Judge, will give me on that great day of His return. And the prize is not just for me but for all who eagerly look forward to his glorious return" (2 Timothy 4:7-8 LASB).

When I thought about losing my mother, and how I grieved my loss. When I thought about my brother, I thought about my grandmother, what she taught us as boys and how she and I didn't want his soul to be lost. When I thought about my grandmother, I thought about my God. I thought about how He brought me. I thought about how He taught me. I thought about who He is. I thought about how He brought me out of pain and suffering so many times throughout the years. I thought about all the times that Jesus dried my tears. I was reminded of His promise, "Weeping may go on all night, but joy comes with the morning" (Psalm 30:5b LASB).

I was reminded that He alone is faithful and that's what makes me grateful for life, family, and friends, those on earth and those in heaven. My thoughts were racing as the clock drew close to seven.

I thought about my godchild, Shantena, and all the times she drove me to doctor's appointments. I thought about life and how sometimes it just doesn't make sense. I thought about Shantena's kind deeds, her needs, and all she does, trying to succeed. It was then that I acknowledged that it is God who supplies our every need. I thought about my friends, Deno/James and Darlene, Dave, Jeanette, the Vaughns, Mary, Ayumi, Erma, Dessie, Doris, Angelique, Angela, Shanelle, Arlene, Kecia and the boys, Eric, the Knapps, Jay, Crawford, Johnny, Booker, Melvin, Quedellis and Lurma, (just to name a few). I thought about my friends, family, the food, visits, and encouraging words and how they so generously gave of themselves and time. I saw so clearly through their deeds, how Jesus had become mine. It was through their love that I heard from heaven above. For in their helping, I realized a little bit of heaven here on earth. Now the time has come to let go of earth and enjoy my new birth . . . . my new life with the Christ. For truly I've gotten to know Him . . . . God.

As I lay a little longer I looked at the clock on the wall. The clock reads the time is now seven. It's time to forget the things of the world and look to heaven then I felt no pain, for I knew within my soul that as the old wounded body dies, there will be many who will cry. But through all the pain, there is much to be gained. Because of my dying, there will be many crying for help and understanding from my God.

I know that without a doubt that one-day they too will see what I see beyond the veil of pain and tears. They will see the man that I've come to know over the years. Yes, they will come to understand more fully about a man worth knowing.

Then all will appreciate this place where I am going, after sowing these words their knowledge will be growing about a man that is worth knowing. The words said as I am dying will no doubt cause crying but will also give the readers life everlasting . . . . "You ought to get to know Him, my Lord and Savior, Jesus Christ. You ought to get to know Him."

So come on all and don't be sad. I know a man who has made me glad . . . Jesus Christ, my Lord and Savior, my deliverer, my doctor, my lawyer, my way maker, my lily of the valley, my bright and shining star. One day you will understand and say "Sherrod, when I die, I want to be where you are. But before I die, I want to get to know Him . . . God, the Lord of Righteousness."

Freed from His Body

For we know that when this tent we live in now is taken down-when we die and leave these bodies-we will have wonderful new bodies in heaven, homes that will be ours forevermore, made for us by God himself, and not by human hands. How weary we grow of our present bodies. That is why we look forward eagerly to the day when we shall have heavenly bodies which we shall put on like new clothes. For we shall not be merely spirits without bodies. These earthly bodies make us groan and sigh, but we wouldn't like to think of dying and having no bodies at all. We want to slip into our new bodies so that these dying bodies will, as it were, be swallowed up by everlasting life. This is what God has prepared for us and, as a guarantee, he has given us his Holy Spirit (II Corinthians 5:1-5 TLBP).

I believe it was Sam Cooke who said, "There have been times when I thought that I wouldn't last for long." Well, there were times when Sherrod's doctors and friends thought he wouldn't last for long, (2 heart attacks, triple BI-pass, amputations, grieving the shut-down of his kidneys with no viable donor, loss of and surviving the grief of his prodigal son) but God gave him strength to carry on. It was a long time coming but his change did come. It was too hard living, but he was not afraid to die, for he knew what was up there beyond the sky. It was a long time coming but his change did come that

September morning when God called him home to be at his side in glory. Hallelujah!!! He no longer had to long for the day to see his grandmother's, mother's or dad's face. For now he had run his race. Imagine if you will, Sherrod walking around heaven all day, two legs and a heart of gold. Oh Happy Day! He's finally free. "For whom the Son sets free is free in deed" "So after he had patiently endured, he obtained the promise (Hebrew 6:15).

Sherrod tried to prepare me for his death. When I talked to him about coming home from the hospital, he changed the subject. I remember saying "I can't wait until you come home." He looked at me and asked, "do you think God is ready for me now?" I responded by saying it was nonsense and that he should think about coming home to his family. His response was that he was ready and not afraid to die because he'd be going to a better place. He looked forward to that better place, just as all Christians do. "Now we look forward with confidence to our heavenly bodies, realizing that every moment we spend in these earthly bodies is time spent away from our eternal home in heaven with Jesus.

We know these things are true by believing, not by seeing. And we are not afraid, but are quite content to die, for then we will be at home with the Lord (II Corinthians 5:6-8 TLB). Sherrod was tired of the race and the battle against diabetes, kidney failure, and amputations. He was weary of the storms, sleepless nights and unsaved souls. He was tired of the hurricanes in his life, his wondering if his children and friends would be all right. He was exhausted by his personal Tsunami, the loss of his toes, feet, legs, and kidneys. He realized that his fight was coming to an end. It is this realization that allowed him to say, "I have fought a good fight. I have finished my course. I have kept the faith. Henceforth there is laid up for me a crown of righteousness, which the Lord, the righteous judge, shall give me at that day: and not to me only, but unto all them also that love his appearing (II Timothy 4:7-8 KJV).

He knew that there was a life much better than the one he was living here on earth. He knew that there was a better home awaiting him. God had protected and kept him and he knew that there was joy awaiting him in heaven. He endured his trials and tribulations for a season and on Saturday, September 17, 2005, while in the hospital, Orville W. Sherrod was chosen to spend eternity with God. He hit his last home run and scored his final touchdown here on earth. I the Lord search the heart, I try the reins, even to give every man according to the fruit of his doings (Jeremiah 17:10, KJV). He now resides with Jesus, sitting at his side.

I am sure he took great pleasure in hearing his Lord and Savior say, "Well done, good and faithful servant; you were faithful over a few things, I will make you ruler over many things. Enter into the joy of your lord (Matthew 25:21 NKJV).

Being free from his body, he went home to get his reward.

The Bible says 'We are confident, I say, and willing rather to be absent from the body, and to be present with the Lord. Wherefore, we labour, that, whether present or absent, we may be accepted of him. For we must all appear before the judgment seat of Christ; that every one may receive the things done in his body, according to that he hath done, whether it be good or bad (2 Corinthians 5:8-10, KJV). Sherrod did the work of an Evangelist and I believe he is blessed in what he did. He lived his faith daily. Even on the day of his death he still proclaimed the goodness of the Lord. He heard the Word of God and obeyed. The day that he was freed from his body, he declared that his work is now ours to do. And so, it is my job and your job to tell your son and my son, too . . . You Ought to Get to Know Him this Mighty God that I serve. He's the King of the Universe.

Yes, my god is Love. He's the only one who can keep you in perfect peace. Take this from someone who knows. You ought to get to know Him . . . Who? God.

SAFE IN HIS ARMS

He will carry the lambs in his arms, holding them close to his heart. He will gently lead the mother sheep with their young (Isaiah 40:11b, LASB). The eternal God is your refuge, and his everlasting arms are under you, He thrusts out the enemy before you (Deuteronomy 33:27a & b).

He walked through the valley of the shadow of death. He did not pitch a tent to stay there. "Yea, though I walk through the valley of the shadow of death, I will fear no evil; for you are with me; your rod and Your staff, they comfort me" (Psalm 23:4 NKJV). Instead of pitching a tent there, he put his trust in God because he knew that God was his only refuge, protector, and deliverer.

There is a poem that I got from a Missionary when I was in East Africa that expresses Sherrod's attitude while he was in the valley of the shadow of death:

> There were times when life was hard to bear: The time Sherrod grieved the loss of his dad and the uncertainty of his son's future; during the first and second heart attacks; when he experienced kidney failure and witnessed friends dying next to him as he sat in the dialysis chair.

Some times were harder than others: The short time when he lost his sight; when he realized just how sick he really was and that physically he would never be the same again. Life was overwhelming and hard to bear the first time the doctor told him he was going to lose his toes. To add to the stress was amputation after amputation, as surgeons chopped away at his body until he had no legs left to stand on. Life was hard each time he lay awake at night in excruciating pain and in the middle of the night when the phantom pains just would not stop. But it was then that he was reminded of how many times God brought him through the pain and sorrow. He looked back over his life and realized all was not lost. All the suffering, grief, disappointments and pain was not in vain. His accomplishments in Christ are what saw him through the hard times. And though he suffered, he understood how and why Christ died on the cross ... just for him and for the hard times that each of us has to go through. Perhaps that is why he never complained. Perhaps that is why he too endured the pain because he wanted others to know that there is strength in God. God strengthened Sherrod enough to call friends and relatives to his bedside before he died. He was able to witness to them one more time before dying. As he died he said these words, "You ought to get to know Him." He used his life and death to show God's love and faithfulness. Truly, Sherrod grew in the valley of death to the point where he felt no pain and no grief.

While in the valley he experienced financial difficulties because his income could not pay the doctor bills, for dialysis or for medicine.

I never let him know but I was concerned because I thought the doctors would refuse care if we didn't have enough money to pay for services.

However, he never worried. He didn't put his trust in money because money couldn't buy him love, health, friends, hope, or salvation. He put his trust in God. There is a song that my mama used to sing and it says, "Some people would rather have houses and land, some would rather have silver and gold. These things they treasure and forget about their souls. I'd rather have Jesus than silver and gold." He wanted and had Jesus and he knew that Jesus would provide. Sherrod was able to "cast all his cares on Jesus because he knew that God cared for him (I Peter 5:7 KJV). He didn't put his trust in fly-by-night pipe dreams, noble causes, his job, or material things because he endured and lost many things. He learned that material things and nobility pass away. At this juncture in his life he knew without a doubt that 'heaven and earth would pass away but Jesus' words will not pass away (Matthew 24:35, KJV). His trust and hope was in Jesus Christ, the lover of his soul, the joy of his salvation. No matter what went on in his life, he knew that he could count on God to keep him from falling. He stood on a solid foundation. He stood on the solid rock of his salvation. Even though Sherrod did not sing as well as some, I believe he kept 2 songs in his heart. One of the songs was one from the 1800's "The solid Rock" by William Bradbury and Edward Mote:

My hope is built on nothing less than Jesus' blood and righteousness; I dare not trust the sweetest frame, but wholly lean on Jesus' name. On Christ the solid Rock I stand, all other ground is sinking sand, all other ground is sinking sand.

When darkness veils His lovely face, I rest on His unchanging grace. In every high and stormy gale, my anchor holds within the veil. On

Christ the solid Rock I stand. All other ground is sinking sand. All other ground is sinking sand.

His oath, His covenant, His blood, support me in the whelming flood. When all around my soul give way, He then is all my hope and stay. On Christ the solid Rock I stand. All other ground is sinking sand. All other ground is sinking sand. When He shall come with trumpet sound, O may I then in Him be found dressed in His righteousness alone, faultless to stand before the throne. Christ the solid Rock I stand. All other ground is sinking sand. All other ground is sinking sand."

The other song was "Jesus you're the center of my Joy." Truly all that's good and perfect comes from God. When Sherrod lost his direction, Jesus was the compass for his way. He was the fire and light when Sherrod's sleepless, painful, nights were long and cold.

He is why Sherrod found pleasure in the simple things in life. In sadness, he was the laughter that shattered all his tears.

When he was all alone, Jesus' hand was there to hold. Because Jesus became Sherrod's everything, he did not worry about current, past, or potential storms of life because he trusted God as his refuge. Living for God gave him a holy boldness. He was proud to be a Christian. He realized that going through the storms was a means of getting to know God. He knew that he couldn't wish or cry away the storms. So he prayed and went through. If you want to get to know Him, God, there are no short cuts. You must go through trials and tribulations. You too must suffer as Jesus Christ suffered. So how did Sherrod come to know Jesus as a mother for the motherless, a father for the fatherless? How did he come to know him as a healer, a heart regulator, a doctor that gives sight to the blind? How did he come to know him as a provider? How did he come to know him as the one who raises the dead? Sherrod suffered and through it all he learned to trust in Jesus. He learned to trust in God.

So when someone asked him who "the son of man is (Matthew 16:13b, NKJV), he could truthfully say as Dr. S. M. Lockridge, from Southern California said:

> God is the one that sits in heaven and reigns on earth. He knows everything we go through and will ever go through in order to get to know Him. He is the one above all others and no matter who is in our lives, God is the most important one. God is worth glorifying when times are good or bad. He is worth praising because he is the one that knows us, sees us and still loves us unconditionally.... in spite of our shortcomings. God is the strong one that keeps us strong with his word. His word keeps us strong in times when most people are weak and fall. He is the one that holds us in the midnight hour when we are lonely and need someone to hold us and comfort us. God is the one that catches us when we feel like we are falling into despair and depression. He is the one that keeps us in perfect peace. When we are sad and feel like we cannot go on and our heads are held low, He is the only one that can lift our heads and our spirits. He is the only true friend that will not complain when we need to talk at midnight. He is the only one that will keep our secrets and not judge or condemn us. God is the only person that we can trust with our deepest fears, hopes and dreams. He is the living God and he is the one that kept Sherrod's mind when he thought he would go crazy worrying about things that God had already

taken care of on the cross. Ultimately, He is God, all knowing, all powerful, all merciful. He is the keeper of our souls.

You ought to get to Know Him. Who? God. Now Sherrod knows Him wholly and completely, face-to-face. Now that he is with Him he can hear Him say "Well done my good and faithful servant. You have been faithful in handling this small amount, so now I will give you many more responsibilities. Let's celebrate together!' (Matthew 25:21b NLT).

Just as God gave Sherrod work to do, He has done the same for you and me. We all have work to do and a short time to do it. Our days are numbered. If we allow Him to, God will direct our path and give us strength to carry out our assignment by using our talents and gifts to do the work He has given us.

God has given us several abilities to realize our assignments. We can do nothing on our own because we have no power other than what God has given us stewardship over. God wants and expects us to increase what He has given us before He returns. Sherrod had little financially and materially because doctor bills exhausted him financially and emotionally.

Nonetheless, he had something more valuable . . . . faith in God and what God could do. He was a broken man . . . broken for God and service. Most importantly, he used what he had for kingdom building. He was a tither of his time, talents, gifts, skills, and money. Sherrod died praising the Lord. He promised God that he would serve Him until the day he died, and he did. He was true to Psalm 146:2 (TLB), "I will praise him as long as I live, yes, even with my dying breath. Sherrod praised and worshipped God on his deathbed. Even then he worked hard to win souls for Christ, now it is your turn.

"Well done my good and faithful servant" (Matthew 25:21b NLT). Sherrod got to know Him. Now . . . You ought to get to know Him. Who? God. That's my king.

REFERENCE BIBLIOGRAPHY

Battle Creek Central Year Book (1967). PEAN, vol. 74. Battle Creek, MI.

Bradbury, W. & Mote, E. (1800). The Solid Rock Great Hymns of the Faith, pg. (272) Singspiration, Inc., Zondeervan Publishing House Grand Rapids, MI.

Eggleston, J. (2008). It's in the Valley we Grow. Retrieved June 8, 2008 from, retrieved June 8, 2008 from http://www.donotgiveup.net.

Holy Bible, King James Version, (Iowa Falls, IA: World Publishing) 1986.

Holy Bible, New Living Translation, (Wheaton, IL: Tyndale House Publishers, Inc.) 1996.

Holy Bible, The Living Bible Paraphrased, (Wheaton, IL: Tyndale Publishers.) 1971.

Life Application Study Bible, New Living Translation, (Wheaton, IL: Tyndale House Publishing, Inc.) 1996.

Lockridge, S.M. That's my King retrieved June 8, 2008, from http://www.bible-commentaries.com.

The Nelson Study Bible, New King James Version, (Nashville, TN: Thomas Nelson Publishers) 1997.